D0431761

CORNERSTONES OF FREEDOM™

WITHDRAWN

The DEMOCRATIC PROCESS

BY MARK FRIEDMAN

CHILDREN'S PRESS®

An Imprint of Scholastic Inc.

New York   Toronto   London   Auckland   Sydney
Mexico City   New Delhi   Hong Kong
Danbury, Connecticut

BRINGING HISTORY to LIFE

Content Consultant
James Marten, PhD
Professor and Chair, History Department
Marquette University
Milwaukee, Wisconsin

Library of Congress Cataloging-in-Publication Data
Friedman, Mark, 1963–
   The democratic process/by Mark Friedman.
      p. cm.—(Cornerstones of freedom)
   Includes bibliographical references and index.
   ISBN-13: 978-0-531-23055-8 (lib. bdg.)   ISBN-10: 0-531-23055-4 (lib. bdg.)
   ISBN-13: 978-0-531-28155-0 (pbk.)   ISBN-10: 0-531-28155-8 (pbk.)
   1. Democracy—United States—Juvenile literature. I. Title. II. Series.
   JK1726.F67 2012
   320.973—dc23   2011031123

No part of this publication may be reproduced in whole or in part, or
stored in a retrieval system, or transmitted in any form or by any means,
electronic, mechanical, photocopying, recording, or otherwise, without
written permission of the publisher. For information regarding permission, write to Scholastic Inc., Attention: Permissions Department, 557
Broadway, New York, NY 10012.

© 2012 Scholastic Inc.

All rights reserved.
Published in 2012 by Children's Press, an imprint of
Scholastic Inc.
Printed in the United States of America 113
SCHOLASTIC, CHILDREN'S PRESS, CORNERSTONES OF FREEDOM™,
and associated logos are trademarks and/or registered trademarks of
Scholastic Inc.

1 2 3 4 5 6 7 8 9 10 R 21 20 19 18 17 16 15 14 13 12

Photographs © 2012: AP Images: 27 (Charles Tasnadi), 23 (Greg Gibson),
25 (Jack Plunkett), 33 (Mark Lennihan), 42 (Marta Lavandier), 20, 58 (Ron
Edmonds), 55 (Stephan Savoia); Corbis Images: 49 (Najlah Feanny), 11
(Stefano Bianchetti); Getty Images: 47 (John Moore), 51 (Mario Tama), 34
(Matthew Cavanaugh), 22 (Pablo Martinez Monisvais); Library of Congress/
Warren K. Leffler: 45; Media Bakery: 4 top, 7, 41; National Archives: 5
top, 6, 29; North Wind Picture Archives: 2, 3, 4, 8, 13, 14, 15, 16, 17, 18, 21,
30, 32, 35, 38, 56, 57 top, 59; PhotoEdit/Peter Byron: 48; Shutterstock, Inc.:
back cover (Gary Blakeley), cover (Thomas Moens); Superstock, Inc.: 36
(Ambient Images, Inc.), 40 (imagebroker.net), 5 bottom, 10 (Universal Images
Group), 28; The Image Works: 24, 50 (Bob Daemmrich), 44 (David R. Frazier),
39 (Scherl/SZ Photo), 37 (Tony Savino); U.S. Department of Defense/Eric
Draper/White House: 57 bottom.

Maps by XNR Productions, Inc.

Did you know that studying history can be fun?

BRING HISTORY TO LIFE by becoming a history investigator. Examine the evidence (primary and secondary source materials); cross-examine the people and witnesses. Take a look at what was happening at the time—but be careful! What happened years ago might suddenly become incredibly interesting and change the way you think!

Contents

A Process for Liberty

IN CONGRESS, JULY 4, 1776.

The unanimous Declaration of the thirteen united States of America,

[text of the Declaration of Independence]

The Declaration of Independence outlines the basic concepts of self-governance that the United States has followed ever since the document's creation.

The Declaration of Independence was based on the idea that individuals have certain rights and that a government cannot take those rights away. Among them are the rights to "life, liberty and the pursuit of happiness." The Constitution of the United States begins with the words "We the people." This emphasizes that the government was formed by the citizens of the country, not by a ruler. The Pledge of Allegiance declares that the U.S. flag represents a nation bound together by the ideas of "liberty and justice for all."

These powerful words carry great weight. They define the United States and its commitment to freedom. But how exactly does the country work to uphold each person's liberty?

U.S. society operates much like a machine with many moving parts. Some of those parts work well together. Some of those parts push against each other. All of those moving parts make up the democratic process. This process is a complex plan for how government works. The plan was laid out in the Constitution more than 200 years ago. It still guides how the machine runs today.

U.S. citizens say the Pledge of Allegiance to show respect for their country.

CHAPTER I

A START-UP REPUBLIC

Members of the Continental Congress signed the Declaration of Independence in 1776.

THE FIRST CONTINENTAL

Congress met in Philadelphia, Pennsylvania, in 1774. Leaders of the 13 American colonies gathered to discuss the problems the colonies faced under the rule of England's king George III. The conflict between the colonies and England soon erupted into violence. The American Revolution began in 1775. The Americans achieved victory in 1783. The Constitution of the United States was **ratified** five years later. The Constitution defined the United States as a **republic**. It would have a representative government.

Thomas Jefferson, George Washington, and Benjamin Franklin were among the Founding Fathers of the United States. They were the leaders and thinkers who created this republic. But these men did not invent all the ideas about the U.S. democratic system on their own. They learned lessons from other societies and thinkers from hundreds and even thousands of years earlier.

Solon was one of the earliest people to promote democratic ideas.

Democracy and Republic

The term **democracy** comes from the Greek word *demokratia*, which means "people rule." In Athens, Greece, a man named Solon (ca. 630–ca. 560 BCE) formed one of the earliest versions of democracy. Solon made laws that took power away from those who were born into it and gave that power to a group of wealthy citizens. He also formed the Ecclesia. This was an assembly where people came to discuss and vote on laws for the society. Not everyone was allowed to participate in the government. But Athens did give more power to more people than many other societies did at the time.

Another important ancient government was the Roman Republic. This government lasted from 509 to 27 BCE. Roman citizens were elected to serve on assemblies. The assemblies were similar to today's lawmaking government bodies. Different parts of the Roman government could overrule each other. This kept any one part of government from becoming more powerful than other parts. This idea later became an important part of the U.S. government.

These ancient societies were unusual because **monarchs** did not control their governments. Power was given to many people instead of just one person. This is the basic idea behind democratic systems such as the one used by the United States.

The Roman senate worked together to make laws and govern the empire.

The Founding Fathers studied the Magna Carta closely. Many ideas in the U.S. Constitution came directly from this document, which was written more than 500 years earlier. Only four copies of the 1215 Magna Carta exist today. Two of these copies are on display at the British Library in England. See page 60 for a link to view the document online.

For many centuries after the governments of ancient Greece and Rome ended, most civilizations were ruled by monarchs. England was the most powerful empire in the world in the early 1200s. But then its monarch's power suffered a blow. King John of England could not stop a rebellion of people demanding fairer treatment. They wanted more control over their own government. King John was forced to sign a document called the Magna Carta on June 15, 1215. The Magna Carta spelled out ways in which England's people would have more freedom under the rule of the king. In time, the English developed a system for government in which powers were divided among the monarch, a prime minister, and a **legislature** called Parliament.

American Quest for Liberty

The quest for liberty in America blossomed in the 1700s. Europeans had been traveling to North America since the late 1400s. England began establishing American colonies in the early 1600s. These settlements existed under the rule of England.

Tensions between England and the colonies rose soon after King George III took the throne in England in 1760. Parliament began passing new taxes on the colonists. But the colonists were not allowed to vote for Parliament members. They felt that it was unfair to be taxed when they didn't have a voice in the government. A breaking point came in 1765 when Parliament enacted the Stamp Act. The law placed a tax on papers such as newspapers and legal documents. The Stamp Act required the colonists to purchase official government stamps for these papers to be legal.

The Stamp Act was met with outrage in the colonies. People launched violent attacks on the government officials who collected the taxes. Great protests erupted

Stamp Act protests sometimes turned into violent riots.

THE FOLLY OF ENGLAND AND THE RUIN OF AMERICA

Victory at the Siege of Yorktown in 1781 secured a U.S. victory in the Revolutionary War.

as colonists argued that the tax was unfair. The colonists rallied around the phrase "No taxation without representation!" The idea that a government should work for the people and with the people's permission became one of the foundations of the American Revolution.

War between Great Britain and the colonies broke out in 1775. The colonists signed the Declaration of Independence on July 4, 1776, and the United States of America was born.

Articles of Confederation

The colonists' joy over the Declaration of Independence was soon replaced with the burden of fighting the war and organizing a new nation. Representatives from all the colonies wrote the Articles of Confederation in 1777. The Articles were a plan for the new United States government. It took four years for every state to approve them. Problems emerged soon after the new government was set up.

The U.S. government's legislature today has two bodies: the House of Representatives and the Senate. But the government's legislature in 1781 had just one body. This single body was very limited in what it could do. The national government could not tax people directly. It instead collected money from state governments. The state governments were responsible for taxing the people. Taxes had been a big issue under British rule. The Founding Fathers did not want a government that could tax the country's people unfairly.

The new government also lacked a president. The colonists did not want any one person to gain too much power in the government. There were also no national

SPOTLIGHT ON

Thomas Paine

Many men wrote inspiring words in favor of revolution during the 1770s. But perhaps no book had a greater impact than Thomas Paine's *Common Sense*. Paine was born in England in 1737. He moved to America in 1774. The revolution was getting started. *Common Sense* made a passionate argument for breaking free from England's rule. It also detailed Paine's ideas for how a new American government should be set up. Paine wrote in plain language that anyone could understand. More copies of *Common Sense* were sold than any other book in the colonies.

courts. All of the courts were at the local or state level. This meant that each state was run differently, which led to disputes between the states.

When the Revolutionary War ended in 1783, the United States needed to begin doing business with other countries. But there was no central authority to represent the nation. Instead, each of the 13 states tried to make their own trade agreements with foreign nations. This proved to be confusing for everyone involved.

Representatives from the United States and Great Britain met in Paris, France, in 1783 to discuss peace terms after the Revolutionary War.

Certain conflicts turned violent. In Massachusetts, a rebellion broke out in 1786. Many local farmers had fallen deep into debt. Some were thrown into prison when they could not pay their debts. Neither the Massachusetts government nor the national government stepped in to help them. Many of the farmers banded together with former soldier Daniel Shays. They staged an armed revolt against the government. It lasted into 1787 before the Massachusetts militia was able to end it.

Shays's Rebellion and other conflicts frightened American leaders into thinking that the young nation was on the verge of collapse. Many of the men who wrote the Articles of Confederation realized they needed a stronger national government. But they also knew that the country's people would not accept a government that was too powerful. Leaders from around the country soon began discussing ideas for a new government.

YESTERDAY'S HEADLINES

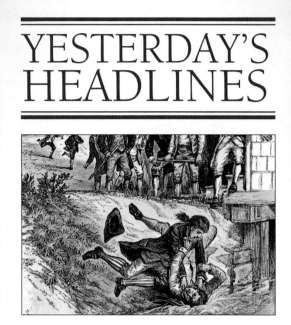

In a February 1787 issue of the *Hampshire Gazette* newspaper, a letter was published expressing outrage at the violent actions of those involved in Shays's Rebellion. This writer believed that it had been fair for Americans to revolt against Great Britain during the war. They had fought against a monarch who ruled them unfairly. But the writer also believed that "the man who dares rebel against the laws of a republic ought to suffer death." The letter captured many Americans' strong feelings about Shays's Rebellion. It revealed that deep divisions had opened in American society during the early years of the country.

CHAPTER 2

POWER to the PEOPLE

Each representative at the Constitutional Convention presented his ideas about how the new government should be organized.

ON MAY 25, 1787, FIFTY-FIVE leaders from across the United States gathered in Philadelphia to begin a long meeting. Many of the most famous leaders of the American Revolution were selected to represent their states. From Virginia, there was George Washington. He had commanded the American forces during the war. At age 81, Benjamin Franklin was the oldest **delegate**. He brought a lifetime of experience as an inventor, writer, thinker, and politician. Not every delegate was famous. The youngest was 26-year-old Jonathan Dayton of New Jersey. Dayton was just beginning a career in politics. He later went on to serve in both the House of Representatives and the Senate. This Constitutional Convention lasted almost five months. It radically changed the United States and the rest of the world.

Government officials are voted into office by U.S. citizens. They represent the citizens' interests.

Representing the People

The key idea behind democracy is that people should have control over their government. The delegates to the Constitutional Convention believed strongly in this concept. But the government they created was not a true democracy. They instead created a republic. In a republic, people elect other citizens to speak and vote for them in government. This is also sometimes called a representative democracy. One of the biggest debates at the convention was over how the people should be represented.

James Madison of Virginia presented a plan for representation. His "Virginia Plan" called for states with more people to get more representatives in Congress. Smaller states argued against the plan. They believed that each state should have just one representative in Congress. Each state would have an equal say in the national government.

SPOTLIGHT ON

James Madison

James Madison had a major impact at the Constitutional Convention. He later went on to play a major role in the new U.S. government. He served as a congressman and as secretary of state. In 1809, he became the fourth president of the United States. But Madison is still best known as the Father of the Constitution. His ideas about representative democracy helped shape the Constitution and the Bill of Rights.

An agreement called the Connecticut Compromise was reached after weeks of debate. The delegates agreed that Congress would be made up of both a House of Representatives and a Senate. The House would follow Madison's plan for giving more representatives to states with more people. But each state would get exactly two representatives in the Senate. The Senate and the House would work separately on creating laws. But they would have to agree on the laws in order for them to be passed.

Separation of Powers

The convention also dealt with another major issue. How would they keep any one part of government from gaining too much power? The national government was very weak under the Articles of Confederation. State governments had a lot of power. This was proving unworkable.

Delegates proposed different ideas for how to solve the problem. Most of these proposals shared the same basic idea. The national government would have three branches. Each branch would have separate powers. This would keep any single branch from having too much power.

Congress, the Supreme Court, and the president all work together to govern the country.

What they came up with is still in force today. The legislative branch is Congress, whose main job is to pass laws. The **executive** branch is led by the president. Its job is to carry out the laws made in Congress. The **judicial** branch is a system of courts. It is headed by the Supreme Court. The judicial branch interprets the Constitution and the laws passed by Congress.

Checks and Balances

The delegates knew that they needed to create rules for how the three branches would work with each other. The nation was especially fearful of the executive branch

TODAY'S PERSPECTIVE

Congress sometimes creates **bills** that have many different parts. The president cannot pick and choose which parts to approve. The whole bill must be either approved or **vetoed**. Many presidents have wanted to take out a red pen and cross out just a few parts of a bill while approving the rest. Congress passed a law in 1996 allowing President Bill Clinton to have a line-item veto. This meant he could cross out parts of bills before signing them into law. But the line-item veto law expired after 18 months. Today, many politicians are calling for it to be restored. They say it is the only reasonable way for a president to approve bills that are hundreds of pages long. Others believe that the line-item veto would give too much power to the president.

Electors meet at their state capitols to cast their votes for president.

gaining too much power. Americans knew that a chief executive was needed to run the nation smoothly. But they feared that one person with too much power could eventually become a monarch.

The delegates wrote a detailed system of checks and balances to prevent any branch from gaining too much control of the government. Checks and balances are rules that allow each branch of government to supervise and even overrule the other branches.

For instance, the Electoral College began as a way to make sure that small states would have an equal say in presidential elections. Citizens vote for representatives called electors. These electors are the ones who actually select the president. The Constitution originally specified that each state received one electoral vote. But the system has changed over time. Larger states now receive more electoral votes.

The legislative branch is another part of the system of checks and balances. This branch creates many bills. But Congress's bills do not become laws without approval from the executive branch. The president reads the bills and either approves or vetoes them. Congress is also checked by the judicial branch. The Supreme Court has the power to review and reject any law created in Congress.

Senators and representatives propose ideas for bills to their fellow legislators and discuss them before voting on those bills.

The judicial branch is kept in check by rules set forth in the Constitution. The president makes selections for new judges to join the Supreme Court. Congress must approve these choices.

The executive branch is subject to its own set of checks and balances. One major check is that Congress can **impeach** the president if he or she commits a crime. The only two presidents ever to be impeached were Andrew Johnson in 1868 and Bill Clinton in 1998. Neither was convicted of crimes nor removed from office.

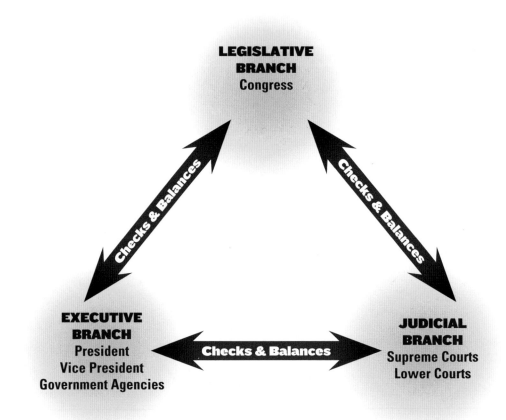

LEGISLATIVE BRANCH
Congress

Checks & Balances

Checks & Balances

EXECUTIVE BRANCH
President
Vice President
Government Agencies

Checks & Balances

JUDICIAL BRANCH
Supreme Courts
Lower Courts

The Struggle to Ratify

The delegates adopted the new Constitution on September 17, 1787. But it still had to be ratified. The delegates decided that at least nine of the 13 states needed to vote in favor of the new Constitution.

Federalists favored the Constitution. They believed in a strong national, or federal, government. They believed that the system of checks and balances was an excellent way to make sure that no single branch of government could gain too much power.

But some Americans felt that a powerful federal government would be a mistake. Many people wanted the individual states to have more power. They especially did not want a

YESTERDAY'S HEADLINES

One of the president's responsibilities is to appoint people to the Supreme Court and the **cabinet**. These people must first be approved by the Senate. Most of the president's choices are approved, even if some members of the Senate have objections. But the Senate sometimes does reject the president's choices. President Ronald Reagan appointed Robert Bork (above) to fill an open seat on the Supreme Court in 1987. Many citizens across the country objected strongly to Bork's nomination. They disagreed with the decisions he had made as a judge. Senators asked Bork questions and eventually rejected him from the Supreme Court.

A FIRSTHAND LOOK AT
THE U.S. CONSTITUTION

The U.S. Constitution begins with the impressive and powerful opening phrase "We the people." It is perhaps the most famous and meaningful single document in the history of government. See page 60 for a link to read it online.

powerful president. The famous politician Patrick Henry said in a 1788 speech, "This Constitution is said to have beautiful features; but when I come to examine these features, sir, they appear to me horribly frightful....Your president may easily become king."

Patrick Henry was known for his passionate speeches.

Most Americans came to embrace federalism as time passed. States ratified the Constitution throughout the winter from 1787 to 1788. Some states continued to object to it. But they agreed to ratify the Constitution as long as there would be **amendments** added to address issues of individual rights. The Constitution was ratified on September 13, 1788. The United States was reborn with a new democratic system.

The Constitution has been the backbone of the U.S. government since its creation.

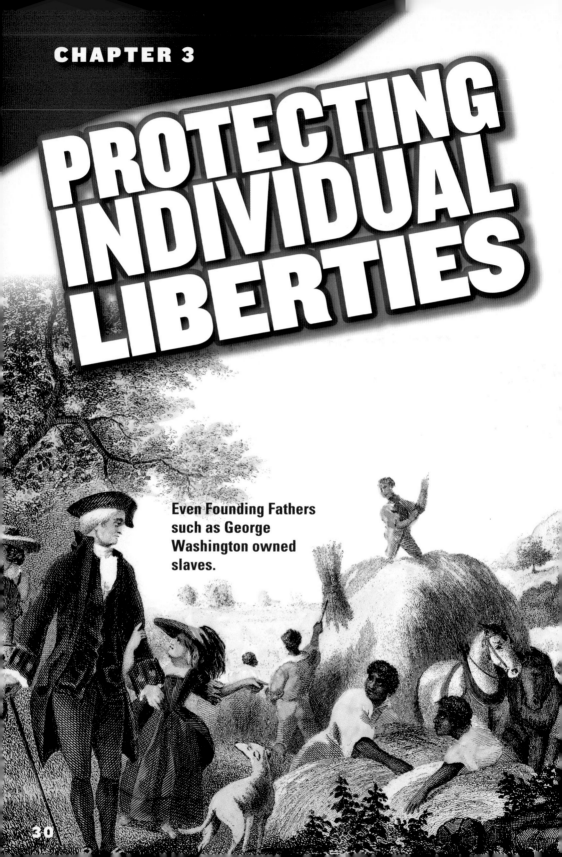

CHAPTER 3

PROTECTING INDIVIDUAL LIBERTIES

Even Founding Fathers such as George Washington owned slaves.

THE UNITED STATES WAS BORN

from the idea of freedom. Yet at the time the Constitution was ratified, the United States itself treated many of its people with greater cruelty than Great Britain had ever shown the colonists. African Americans had lived in the United States for centuries, but most were slaves. They had no freedoms at all. The truth is that the Constitution did not provide liberty to all people. Many signers of the Constitution attempted to ban slavery. But others were slave owners. It would be more than a century before slavery ended.

Even while slavery existed, the country was built around a belief in individual liberties. The Constitution spells out specific rules for how the government must protect this freedom. Debates over individual rights have continued ever since the nation's founding.

The idea of human rights was changed forever when King John signed the Magna Carta.

What Are Individual Rights?

One of the most important ideas in the Magna Carta was that all human beings have rights. All people are free. No free person can be imprisoned without a fair trial. This idea may seem obvious to us today. We benefit from living in a republic that has recognized the basic rights of individuals for more than two centuries. People are free to work in jobs they desire. They are free to keep the money they earn. They are free to practice their own religions. They are free to live as they please.

The Declaration of Independence famously declares that all people have the right to "life, liberty and the pursuit of happiness." Today, most people around the world agree that every human has those rights. They also have the rights to receive equal treatment, own property, and more.

Adding to the Constitution

The language of the Constitution allows for changes, called amendments, to be added. The framers recognized that the government needed a way to change with the times. An amendment must be approved by

U.S. citizens are allowed to spend their money however they want to.

A FIRSTHAND LOOK AT
THE BILL OF RIGHTS

The first 10 amendments to the Constitution were written as one document called the Bill of Rights. It was ratified on December 15, 1791. See page 60 for a link to read the Bill of Rights online.

two-thirds of both the Senate and the House. Then the states vote on it. An amendment becomes law if three-quarters of the states approve it.

Some Federalists thought it was a bad idea to name specific individual rights in the Constitution. They believed that if only certain rights were listed, then the

Members of Congress often debate new bills for many weeks or months before voting on them.

George Mason's 1776 Declaration of Rights was one of the inspirations for the Bill of Rights.

government might act as if those were the only rights people had. This could allow the government to take away other rights that had not been named in the Constitution. But certain states insisted on amendments that guaranteed individual rights.

The Bill of Rights

Leaders began working on the first set of amendments even before the Constitution was ratified. In 1791, the first 10 amendments were ratified together as the Bill of Rights.

The First Amendment might be the most important one of all. It includes the rights to freedom of religion, free speech, a free press, and many other freedoms.

Freedom of religion had been a major issue in colonial times. Great Britain banned all religions other than Anglicanism. People had fled to the American colonies seeking the freedom to practice their own religions.

People practice a wide variety of religions in the United States.

The freedoms of speech and the press mean that the government cannot stop individuals from saying or writing whatever they want to. These also guarantee that newspapers can publish anything they want to.

Some of the other amendments in the Bill of Rights protect individual rights such as the right to own weapons (Second Amendment), freedom from being arrested or searched by police without probable cause (Fourth Amendment), and the right to a quick and fair trial by jury (Sixth Amendment).

Police officers need special permission from a judge to search someone's home.

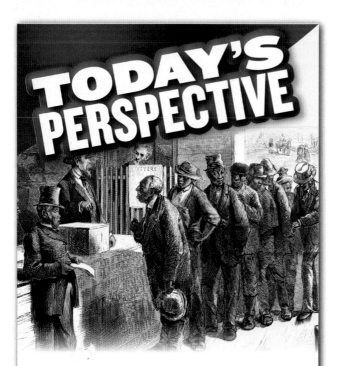

Today, the individual rights of all people are protected by law. But the original Constitution failed to provide rights for African American slaves and other minority groups. It was not until the 13th Amendment was passed in 1865 that the United States banned slavery. But African Americans continued to suffer even after the amendment was passed. Individual states passed laws that treated African Americans poorly. Today, many states have taken measures to apologize for slavery and other unfair laws of the past. Virginia's state government passed a resolution in 2007 that officially expressed regret for the state's past history of slavery. Many other states have made similar apologies.

The American people changed their opinions on many issues as years passed. Some issues were so important that further amendments to the Constitution were needed. There have been 27 amendments so far. The 13th Amendment guarantees that slavery "shall [not] exist within the United States." The 14th Amendment guarantees civil rights to all U.S. citizens. The 15th Amendment assures all men the right to vote regardless of "race, color, or previous condition of servitude." This meant that former slaves could vote. The 18th Amendment banned alcohol from being sold, but the 21st Amendment allowed

Police officers destroyed large amounts of alcohol after the 18th Amendment was passed.

alcohol to be sold again. The 19th Amendment gave women the right to vote.

Clashing Rights

The rights of an individual can come into conflict with those of other individuals or a larger community. Many people may want to behave in ways that would harm others. An individual's rights may have to be given up in these cases.

For instance, the First Amendment guarantees the freedom of speech. But laws also place limits on this freedom. Individuals are not allowed to harm others by telling lies about them. The press is not allowed to knowingly publish lies.

Culture and technology have changed greatly since the Constitution was written. The freedom of the press now also applies to radio, television, and the Internet. The freedom of speech includes the freedom to express oneself in music, drama, and other art forms. The U.S. Supreme Court ruled in 2011 that a California law

As technology continues to change and new technologies are invented, the Constitution may change as well.

banning the sale of violent video games was unconstitutional. The court judged that it is more important to uphold the game creators' right to free speech than it is to protect children from violent games.

Not all Americans agree with such attitudes. They argue for stricter controls on freedom of speech. The same types of debates continue about many other rights guaranteed in the Bill of Rights. But what remains true from the 1700s is that the system established in the Constitution is the same. The Constitution can be amended if the nation's opinions change dramatically about certain issues. It has already happened many times and will happen again.

SPOTLIGHT ON

The Second Amendment

The Second Amendment is one of the most heavily debated parts of the Constitution. It assures that individuals have the right to own weapons. It states that people need weapons in order to maintain "a well regulated militia . . . necessary to the security of a free State." Opponents of gun ownership believe that people no longer need to own weapons. Militias are a thing of the past. Today's guns are more powerful than those of the past. But many Americans still believe that gun ownership is an important right. As recently as 2010, the Supreme Court ruled on a case upholding the Second Amendment. But it remains a controversial issue for many Americans.

CHAPTER 4

CHALLENGES to the DEMOCRATIC PROCESS

In the 2000 U.S. presidential election, Florida election officials recounted the votes by hand.

THE 2000 U.S. PRESIDENTIAL

election pitted Republican candidate George W. Bush against Democrat Al Gore. The election was very close. Gore won the popular vote. More citizens voted for him than for Bush. But the popular vote is only to choose Electoral College representatives for each state. The candidates were separated by just 20 electoral votes after most of the states were decided. One state, however, was too close to call. Florida had 25 electoral votes. It could swing the election to either candidate. The state's final count showed that Bush had just a few hundred more votes than Gore. But a result that close requires all the votes to be recounted to catch any errors. An intense struggle broke out over how the votes would be recounted. Bush eventually won the state by just 537 votes and became president.

U.S. citizens vote in private booths so that other people cannot see who they are voting for.

Free and Fair Elections

There are more than 313 million American citizens. Only 537 Americans are elected to represent them in the federal government. There are 435 members of the House of Representatives and 100 senators. The president and vice president are also elected. This means the American people must trust in their elected officials. They also must be able to trust that the way in which officials are elected is free and fair.

It took centuries for the republic to correct itself and guarantee all American citizens the right to vote. In theory, elections are free and fair. But the 2000 presidential election showed that the fairness of elections is sometimes challenged. Democrats across the nation voiced their protests when the Florida votes were recounted and George Bush was declared the winner. They complained that some votes were not recounted. Surrounding all of this controversy was the reality that Al Gore had won the popular election. But Bush became president because he won the electoral vote. This seemed like an unfair outcome to Democrats. It caused many Americans to question the electoral voting system.

SPOTLIGHT ON

Voting Rights

One basic individual right that some Americans have struggled to achieve is the right to vote. The 15th Amendment gave African American men the right to vote in 1870. The 19th Amendment gave women voting rights in 1920. But these constitutional amendments did not immediately remove all boundaries. Some local governments required voters to pass reading tests to prove they could vote. These laws were a way of keeping many uneducated African Americans from voting. Under President Lyndon Johnson (above), Congress passed the Voting Rights Act in 1965. It finally removed all barriers to voting for any Americans. This is an excellent example of the democratic system correcting itself. Individual rights were being denied at the local level. The federal government provided a solution.

Wartime Powers

The United States entered a period of war soon after Bush was elected president. Wartime powers can be one of the most stressful challenges to a republic. One of the president's main duties is to serve as commander in chief of the U.S. military. A group of terrorists attacked the United States on September 11, 2001. The terrorists hijacked airplanes and crashed them into important buildings. Thousands of Americans were killed in the attack. President Bush immediately declared a "war on terror." He promised to root out the terrorist leaders.

The president, his staff, and the military began a campaign to find terrorists by listening to people's

A VIEW FROM ABROAD

Foreign nations had a range of reactions to the 2000 presidential election. U.S. elections are an important symbol of the democratic process in action. Some outside observers were alarmed by the odd nature of how electoral votes are counted. A reporter for the French newspaper *La Croix* wrote, "Can we laugh at the US? The answer is yes, of course, but not too much. . . . The danger would be to throw out the democracy baby with the bath water of the US electoral system." Others praised Americans for remaining calm during the election crisis. One Russian citizen praised the United States for its stability. He noted that in Russia, "Something like this could lead to disaster."

Many suspected terrorists were held at the Guantanamo Bay U.S. Naval Station in Cuba after the attacks of September 11, 2001.

phone calls and intercepting their e-mails. Those suspected of being terrorists were held in military prisons for long periods of time without being brought to trial. Americans were shocked when photographs of U.S. soldiers torturing suspected terrorists were leaked to the public. The photographs proved that the U.S. military had gone beyond its authority.

The Constitution states that the president and Congress have certain extra powers in times of war. But many Americans believed that President Bush went too far in denying rights to individuals. They believed that it was a threat to democracy when the government took such severe action.

A FIRSTHAND LOOK AT
THE USA PATRIOT ACT

On October 26, 2001, President George W. Bush signed the USA PATRIOT Act into law. The controversial act expanded the government's rights to search American citizens for signs of terrorist activity. See page 60 for a link to view the document online.

Inequality

It does not always take a major event to create challenges to the democratic process. Some challenges exist every day. Critics of American society point to the increasing gap between the very rich and the very poor in the

Many U.S. citizens live in poor conditions.

Schools in less wealthy areas of the United States are often overcrowded.

United States. They believe that the federal government is not equipped to solve the issue. More than 46 million Americans were living in poverty in 2011.

Poverty is an example of inequality, in which one group in society lives in worse conditions than the majority. Another example of inequality in today's society is the growing number of citizens without proper health care. Also, some public schools are poorly funded, leading to poor education for many children. Another problem is the technology gap. Many Americans benefit

Some students have access to technology such as cell phones and computers, but many do not.

from computers, cell phones, and Internet access. But other groups are left behind because they cannot afford this technology.

Are inequalities like these actually caused by a democratic system? Some people argue that the U.S. government does not have the ability to prevent or solve inequalities because its powers are so limited. They want government to take more control of social problems. For instance, the federal government has considered creating national health care coverage for all citizens. Critics argue that such a plan is not appropriate in a democratic system. They believe it gives too much control to the government.

On the other hand, some Americans have argued in recent years that government already has too much control. They believe the federal government has grown too large, taxes its citizens too heavily, and has taken away too many rights. These people say that we have moved too far away from the limited government mapped out by the Founding Fathers.

The debate over national health care coverage continues to be an important social and political issue in the United States.

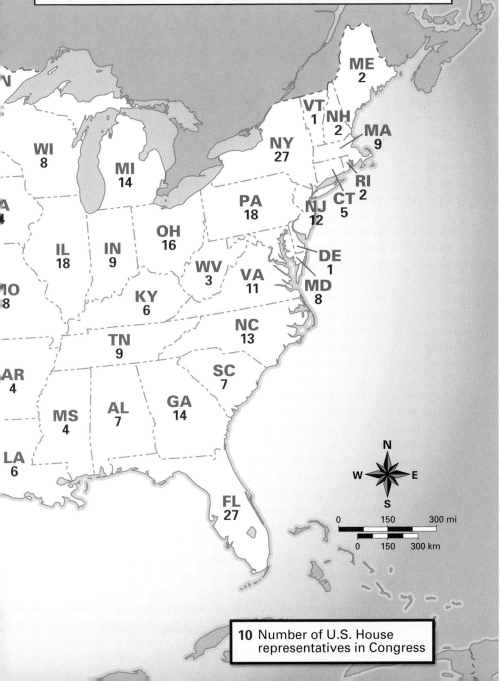

Congress is structured with two chambers: the House of Representatives and the Senate. Each state sends two representatives (senators) to the Senate. In the House, the number of representatives for each state depends on the size of the state's population. Congress originally had representatives from just 13 states. But the map has changed as the nation has grown and as state populations have shifted. There are now 50 states and 435 members in the House of Representatives.

ME
2

VT
1

NH
2

MA
9

NY
27

RI
2

WI
8

MI
14

PA
18

NJ
12

CT
5

OH
16

DE
1

IL
18

IN
9

WV
3

VA
11

MD
8

MO
8

KY
6

NC
13

TN
9

AR
4

SC
7

MS
4

AL
7

GA
14

LA
6

FL
27

N
W — E
S

| 0 | 150 | 300 mi |

| 0 | 150 | 300 km |

10 Number of U.S. House representatives in Congress

Of the People, By the People, For the People

The democratic system creates government for the people. Democratic governments serve and protect their citizens. But citizens also have responsibilities they must take seriously to keep the system running smoothly and effectively.

Most citizens contribute to the democratic system by working to earn pay. Some of that pay goes to the government as taxes. Work also contributes as a creative and productive force that moves the nation forward. It is not government's responsibility to grow food, invent new products, or run factories. It is up to citizens. It is also the citizens' responsibility to live by the law. Lying, cheating, stealing, and committing violent acts are all crimes that can destroy a free society.

In times of war, the government cannot provide a ready-made army. Instead, citizens serve in the armed

IN 1870, THE 15TH AMENDMENT GAVE

forces and work to protect the nation. Voting is both a right and a responsibility. It allows citizens to place representatives with whom they agree into positions of power. But they can end up with poor leaders if they do not vote wisely. By fulfilling these and other responsibilities, the people of the United States can ensure that the democratic process continues to work smoothly and ensure freedom for all.

U.S. citizens must carefully consider each candidate's ideas before deciding whom to vote for.

AFRICAN AMERICAN MEN VOTING RIGHTS.

Thomas Paine

Benjamin Franklin (1706–1790) was a politician, inventor, author, and statesman. He was an influential voice in founding the United States government. He was one of just six men who signed both the Declaration of Independence and the Constitution.

George Washington (1732–1799) became a military hero after leading the Continental army in the Revolutionary War. He was unanimously elected as the first president of the United States after the Constitution was ratified.

Patrick Henry (1736–1799) was a politician who served as governor of Virginia during the Revolutionary War. He was a fiery speaker who made bold, controversial statements. His vocal objections to the Stamp Act led to some of the earliest actions toward revolution.

Thomas Paine (1737–1809) was a writer and supporter of the revolutionary cause. His 1776 book *Common Sense* offered an inspired defense of the war against Great Britain. During the war, he wrote a series of articles called *The Crisis*, which were also widely read and inspired the nation to continue its fight.

King George III (1738–1820) took the throne of England upon his father's death in 1760. He was a hero in Great Britain for his support of the British efforts to put down the American colonists. He was hated in America.

Thomas Jefferson (1743–1826) was the author of the Declaration of Independence and one of the most inspirational leaders of the revolutionary era. He was elected as the third president of the United States in 1800. He oversaw the Louisiana Purchase, which expanded the borders of the United States to the west.

James Madison

Daniel Shays (ca. 1747–1825) was an American soldier in the Revolutionary War who returned to his Massachusetts farm to find himself in debt. He lost his farm and organized other farmers in the same situation to revolt against the local government, which would not assist them. Shays's Rebellion grew into an armed conflict with the Massachusetts militia.

James Madison (1751–1836) was called the Father of the Constitution for his active leadership role at the Constitutional Convention and for his part in writing *The Federalist*. He later served as secretary of state under President Thomas Jefferson and became the fourth president in 1809.

George W. Bush

George W. Bush (1946–) was the 43rd president of the United States. His presidency was dominated by war against foreign terrorists, which he began after the 9/11 attacks on several U.S. cities in 2001, less than a year into his first term of office.

TIMELINE

1215

The Magna Carta is signed in England.

1760

King George III takes the throne in England.

1765

Parliament imposes the Stamp Act on the American colonies.

1776

The United States is born with the signing of the Declaration of Independence.

1788

The Constitution is ratified.

1791

The Bill of Rights is ratified.

1865

The 13th Amendment ends slavery in the United States.

1868

The 14th Amendment guarantees citizenship rights to former slaves.

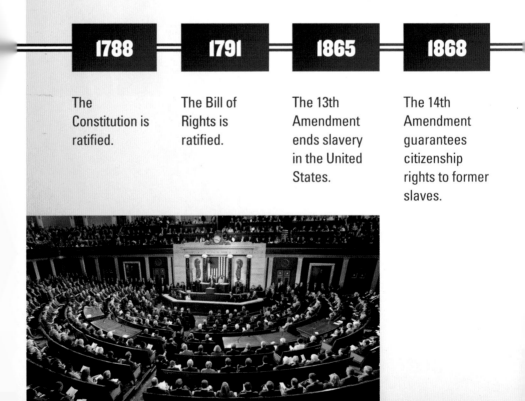

1783

The Revolutionary War ends.

1786–1787

Shays's Rebellion in Massachusetts leads to an armed conflict between citizens and the state militia.

1787

The Constitutional Convention meets in Philadelphia.

1870

The 15th Amendment guarantees voting rights to men of all races.

1919

The 18th Amendment bans the manufacturing and selling of alcohol.

1920

The 19th Amendment gives women the right to vote.

2000

The presidential election is decided with a controversial recount of the votes in Florida.

LIVING HISTORY

Primary sources provide firsthand evidence about a topic. Witnesses to a historical event create primary sources. They include autobiographies, newspaper reports of the time, oral histories, photographs, and memoirs. A secondary source analyzes primary sources, and is one step or more removed from the event. Secondary sources include textbooks, encyclopedias, and commentaries.

The Bill of Rights The original document containing the Bill of Rights is on display at the National Archives in Washington, D.C. This museum houses many other key documents in American history. You can also view the Bill of Rights online by visiting *www.archives.gov /exhibits/charters/bill_of_rights.html*

The Magna Carta Of the four existing copies of the Magna Carta, two are held by the British Library in London, England. To see a close-up view with translations, visit *www.bl.uk/treasures/magnacarta /document/index.html*

The USA PATRIOT Act In order to gain more powers to fight the war against terrorism, President George W. Bush urged Congress to pass the USA PATRIOT Act. It became law on October 26, 2001. The act gave law enforcement organizations the power to spy on U.S. citizens and tightened border security, among other measures. To read the full text of the act, visit *http://epic.org/privacy/terrorism /hr3162.html*

The U.S. Constitution The Constitution of the United States can be seen in person at the National Archives in Washington, D.C. You can also view the original document online by visiting *www.archives .gov/exhibits/charters/constitution.html*

RESOURCES

Books

Fradin, Dennis B. *The Bill of Rights*. Tarrytown, NY: Marshall Cavendish Benchmark, 2009.

Han, Lori Cox, and Tomislav Han. *Handbook to American Democracy*. New York: Facts on File, 2011.

Landau, Elaine. *The 2000 Presidential Election*. New York: Children's Press, 2002.

O'Donnell, Liam. *Democracy*. Mankato, MN: Capstone Press, 2008.

Travis, Cathy. *Constitution Translated for Kids*. Austin, TX: Ovation Books, 2010.

Web Sites

Our Documents

www.ourdocuments.gov/

This official government Web site explores 100 key documents related to democracy and U.S. history, including the Declaration of Independence, the Articles of Confederation, the Constitution, and the Bill of Rights.

The White House—Our Government

www.whitehouse.gov/our-government

The White House's official site includes pages that explain the three branches of the federal government, the Constitution, and more.

Visit this Scholastic Web site for more information on the democratic process: www.factsfornow.scholastic.com

GLOSSARY

amendments (uh-MEND-muhnts) changes that are made to a law or a legal document

bills (BILLZ) written plans for new laws

cabinet (KAB-uh-nit) a group of high-ranking government officials who advise the president on important issues

delegate (DEL-i-git) representative to a convention or congress

democracy (di-MAH-kruh-see) a form of government in which people choose their leaders in elections

executive (eg-ZEK-yuh-tiv) the part of government that carries out laws, or the person in charge of that department

Federalists (FED-ur-uhl-ists) members of a U.S. political party that supported a strong federal government

impeach (im-PEECH) bring formal charges against a public official for misconduct

judicial (joo-DISH-uhl) relating to the court system

legislature (LEJ-iss-lay-chur) the part of government that is responsible for making and changing laws

monarchs (MAH-narks) people who rule countries, such as kings or queens

ratified (RAT-uh-fyed) agreed to or approved officially

republic (ri-PUHB-lik) a form of government in which the people have the power to elect representatives who manage the government

vetoed (VEE-tohd) stopped a bill from becoming a law

INDEX

Page numbers in *italics* indicate illustrations.

ABOUT THE AUTHOR

Mark Friedman has been a writer and editor of children's books and educational materials for 20 years. He has written books on history, politics, government, science, religion, and sports as well as textbooks and other classroom materials. Mark lives with his family near Chicago, Illinois.

31901051058016